A DAY IN THE LIFE OF AN
Actress

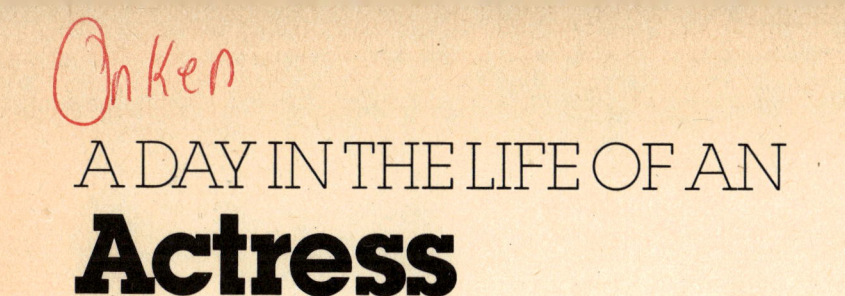

by Betsy Smith
Photography by F. Reid Buckley, Jr. and Marianne Bernstein

Troll Associates

Library of Congress Cataloging in Publication Data

Smith, Betsy Covington.
    A day in the life of an actress.

    Summary: Follows the activities of an actress during a typical working day.
    1. Hannah, Page—Juvenile literature. 2. Actors—United States—Biography—Juvenile literature.
[1. Hannah, Page. 2. Actors and actresses. 3. Occupations] I. Buckley, F. Reid, ill. II. Title.
PN2287.H2S65   1985   792'.028'0924 [B]   84-8678
ISBN 0-8167-0105-9 (lib. bdg.)
ISBN 0-8167-0106-7 (pbk.)

Copyright © 1985 by Troll Associates, Mahwah, New Jersey.
All rights reserved. No part of this book may be used or reproduced in any manner whatsoever without written permission from the publisher.
Printed in the United States of America.

10 9 8 7 6 5 4 3 2 1

The author and publisher wish to thank Page Hannah for her cooperation. We also wish to express our thanks to Lee Fryd of NBC Television, and the cast and crew of *Search for Tomorrow,* for their generous assistance and cooperation. Thanks also to Murphy Alexander, Marjorie Stern and Midge Richardson, editor at *Seventeen* magazine.

Cover photograph and photographs on pages 16, 17, 18, 19, 20, 21, 22, 23, 24, 25 by Marianne Bernstein. Photograph on page 7 by Carlo Meconi for *Seventeen* magazine. Photograph on page 15 courtesy of Paramount Pictures Corporation. Balance of photography by F. Reid Buckley, Jr.

At six-thirty in the morning the alarm clock rings. Page Hannah would like to stay in bed, but she knows she can't. To become a successful actress, she must make every minute of each day count. So she dresses quickly and goes outside to warm up for her morning run.

Keeping fit is vital for any actor or actress. Acting is a very competitive career, and success often goes to those who have the most stamina and work the hardest. After she finishes jogging, Page stops to pick up her breakfast. She will eat at home while getting ready for what she knows will be a very busy day.

Just before nine o'clock, Page arrives at the executive offices of *Seventeen* magazine. Like many other actresses, Page accepts modeling jobs as well as acting assignments if she can work them into her schedule. She began working as a model for *Seventeen* when one of the magazine's talent scouts—who was looking for redheads—spotted her on the street.

Since Page has been photographed for *Seventeen* several times, the editors of the magazine know her well. Page shows the senior editor and a staff member some new additions to her portfolio. She also discusses the possibility of further work for the magazine.

Some of the photographs that were taken of Page for a feature in *Seventeen* have just arrived at the executive offices. Hundreds of photos were taken, but only one will be used. The background of the photographs is blank because the picture will be fitted into a prepared magazine spread, complete with type.

When Page leaves the magazine's offices, she hurries uptown. Shortly before ten-thirty she arrives at the university where she takes her acting classes. After four years here, she will earn a college degree. Acting is Page's great love, but she knows that finishing her education is just as important.

Before going into class, Page phones her answering service to get her messages. She checks in regularly in case a casting director has called to offer her one of the parts she has auditioned for recently. But today, only her manager has called, reminding her that they have an appointment later in the afternoon.

Today's first class is a scene-study class. Different groups of students perform scenes that they have rehearsed outside of class. As each group performs, the other students pay close attention. After each performance, the instructor comments on how the performers might improve the scene.

Page's group performs the next scene. Sometimes scenes are chosen from well-known plays, and sometimes they are simple skits the group has developed from ideas suggested in class. Acting classes are not just for beginners. Even well-established actors brush up on their craft by taking classes.

Next on Page's schedule is her jazz dance class. When she arrives, most of the other students are already there. She quickly changes into her leotard and begins her warm-up exercises. Warming up helps prevent strained muscles.

Dancing is an important part of Page's overall training. It teaches her to move quickly and gracefully on stage. An actress who can dance has an advantage over actresses who have no dance training. This is true not only because some parts involve dancing, but also because dance training builds poise and self-confidence.

After dance class, Page meets a friend for lunch. He attends the same university, but they do not have any classes together. Since Page has such a busy schedule, lunch is usually the only time she has to spend with friends during the day. She can hardly wait to show off what's inside her portfolio.

One of the photographs she has with her was taken on the set of a movie in which she acted. Working with a top director and well-known actors, she gained invaluable experience and learned that shooting a film requires a real team effort. Everyone must work together to get the film finished quickly and professionally.

Right after lunch, Page moves on to the most important part of her day. She recently began a regular part in a daytime television drama. At the network television studio, she rushes from the hair stylist to the wardrobe department and then back to her dressing room, where she begins putting on the first touches of her make-up.

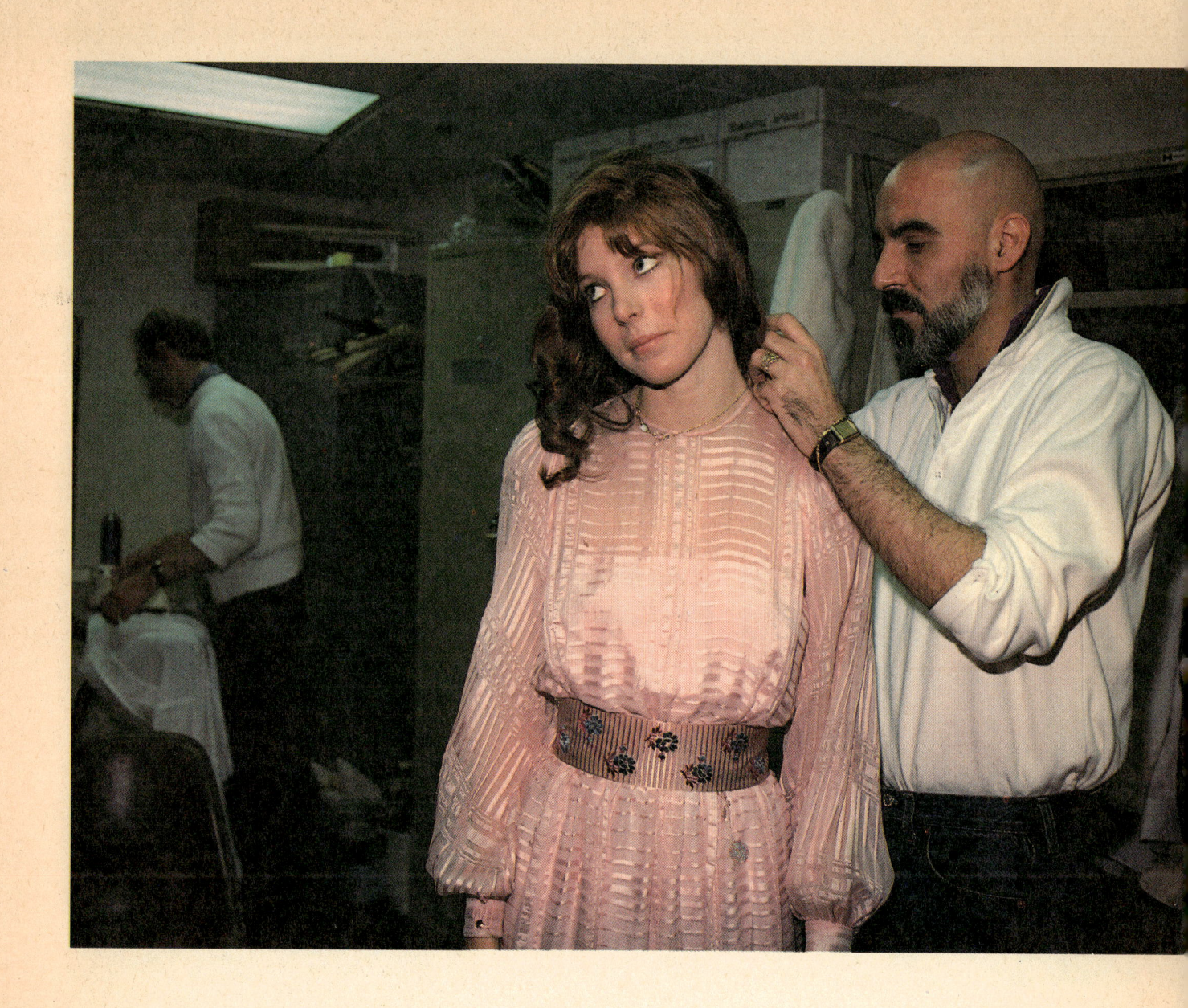

Page puts on the dress she will wear for today's taping and stops in to see the wardrobe supervisor. His job is to make sure the dress each actress is wearing fits her properly. This means he must make quick last-minute alterations if they are needed. Today, he pins the collar of Page's dress so the neckline will look just right.

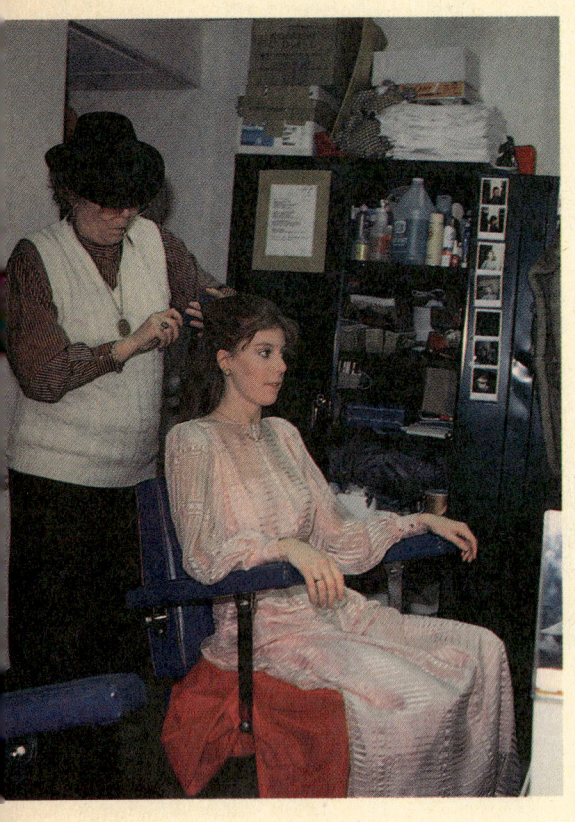

After Page finishes with wardrobe, she goes back to the hair stylist. Since daytime television dramas are "continuing stories," it is important for each actress to look the same as she did when the show ended the day before. So the stylist takes great care with Page's hair.

Getting ready for a daily television role is a big job. Page's next visit is with the make-up artist, who must make each actor and actress look natural under the bright lights used for color videotaping. The make-up artist gets help from an assistant, but usually puts the finishing touches on each member of the cast himself.

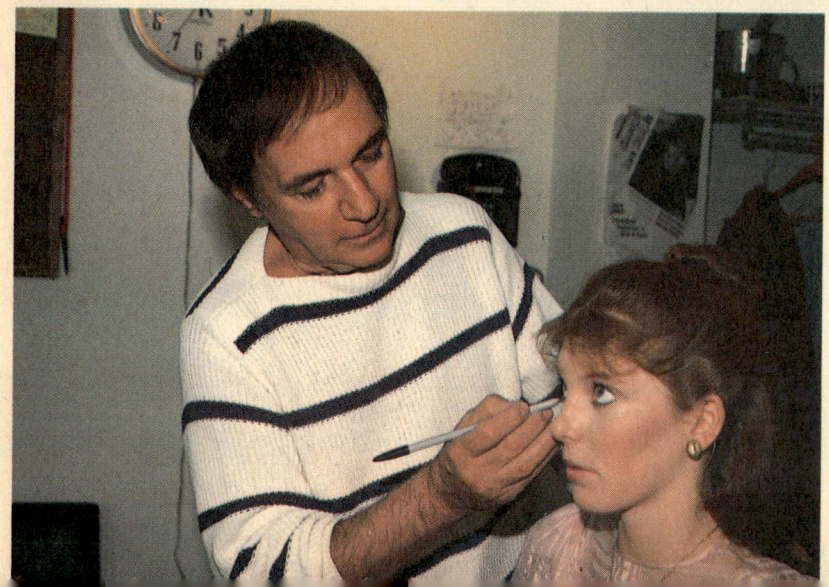

When her make-up is finished, Page takes a few minutes to review her script. In a videotaping session, a missed cue or forgotten line is not quite as serious as in a "live" performance. But each mistake means part of the scene may have to be redone. This takes time and adds to a show's production costs.

While Page waits in the actors' lounge, she has a chance to watch herself in the episode she taped the day before. Before long, the phone rings. Page and another actress are asked by an assistant director to come onto the set.

On the set, Page gets final touchups from the hair stylist and the make-up artist. This is done because the lights are bright enough so that a stray hair or an uneven application of make-up will show up on camera. Page is impressed by the level of perfection demanded by network programs.

At last the taping of Page's scene begins. In the story, she drops by to visit her brother, who is played by one of the program's leading actors. Since the character Page plays is new to the series, much of the dialogue helps explain who she is and what her life has been like.

Suddenly the assistant director interrupts the scene. Through his headset, he is in constant communication with the director in the control room. The director feels that Page's entrance scene is too long. So the assistant director instructs the actors to drop a few lines of dialogue to shorten the scene.

The scene begins again. Page's brother introduces her to the woman he plans to marry. But, in keeping with the traditions of daytime drama, Page knows a secret that could destroy the couple's relationship. Viewers will not find out about that secret until the next episode.

25

After taping the TV show, Page takes a bus to her manager's office. He is responsible for guiding her career. Although Page is pleased with her daytime television role, she is also looking for parts in the theater and in films. So she keeps her portfolio up to date. It contains photographs and information sheets listing her professional acting experience.

Page's manager greets her warmly and tells her about a new play that is being cast. He feels that one particular part in the play would be a perfect role for Page. After showing her the script and discussing the play, he arranges for Page to audition that afternoon.

Page arrives a little early at the rehearsal studio where the audition is taking place. As always, she gets just a little nervous as she waits her turn. What will the audition be like? Will she be asked to do a monologue from memory? She takes several deep breaths to calm herself.

On the rehearsal stage, Page reads for the part in front of the play's director and casting director. She is one of many actresses to read for this part today. Page senses that the directors are less than enthusiastic about the way she creates the character.

When she leaves the audition, Page is not pleased with her effort. It's been such a busy day for her that she may well have lost the edge she needed to get the part. She decides to walk several blocks back to her apartment rather than take a bus. Page hopes that walking will help her shake off the tension that has built up over the day.

Soon after she gets home, Page is visited by her friend Amy. They attend the same acting class, and they must work on a scene. While they are rehearsing, the phone rings. It is the casting director from the play Page auditioned for. He wants her to come back for a second audition. Page is surprised and pleased. Apparently she had done well after all!

Later that night, Page attends a private screening of the film she worked on last summer. She is nervous and excited, but that's part of the magic of an acting career. After long hours of classes and study, tryouts and call-backs, and endless hours of rehearsals, it's always a thrill to see your name on the screen. And it makes all the hard work worthwhile.